BLUFF YOUR WAY
IN
SMALL BUSINESS

JOHN
WINTERSON RICHARDS

ℛℛ

RAVETTE PUBLISHING

Published by Ravette Publishing Limited
P.O. Box 296
Horsham
West Sussex RH13 8FH

Telephone: (01403) 711443
Fax: (01403) 711554

First printed 1992
Reprinted 1993, 1994
Revised 1997
Reprinted 1998

Series Editor – Anne Tauté

Cover design – Jim Wire, Quantum
Printing & binding – Cox & Wyman Ltd.
Production – Oval Projects Ltd.

The Bluffer's Guides® series is based
on an original idea by Peter Wolfe.

An Oval Project
for Ravette Publishing.

CONTENTS

THE MISSION

The Professional Game

Sooner or later the true bluffer will end up heading his or her own Small Business.

There are two reasons* for this:

1. For the compulsive bluffer, Small Business is the only game in town. Where an amateur bluffs only for slight social advantage, the bluffer in business will stake everything – money, home, family, future – on his or her abilities.

2. Small Business is the bluffer's home ground. Here at last, for reasons that will soon be explained, is an activity where the art of bluff is not merely a useful optional extra but the decisive factor which determines success or failure. Small Business is 99 per cent bluff (opinions differ about what exactly constitutes the other 1 per cent).

Of course, the title 'Small Business' is something of a misnomer. No bluffer particularly wants to head a **small** business. He or she would probably prefer to own a **big** business. Alas, it is a great social injustice that few are able to go straight in at their preferred level. For

---

*In business there should be two reasons for everything: two separate explanations ready to justify any decision. Ideally one should be hard and commercial, the other more esoteric. Anyone disposed to argue with the decision will not know which is the real reason, so if attacked on commercial grounds, you will hint it was really an esoteric decision, and vice versa.

most, the best way to own one's own big business is to
start with a small one and make it bigger. And the
best way of doing that is to convince everyone that
the small business is already a big business.

In fact, if a small business is to stand any chance at
all, it is not merely desirable, but essential, that it
appears to be what it hopes to become.

The beginning of small business wisdom is this: no
matter how much people profess to admire it, *everyone
hates small business*.

This is because:

Customers feel safer buying from the firms everyone
else buys from.

Suppliers are reluctant to grant easy credit terms to
those who are less likely to buy regularly or in bulk.

Taxmen and other bureaucrats enjoy picking on
those who cannot afford the top division advisers they
fear.

Bankers consider Third World governments who
regularly default on large loans to be better credit
risks than small businesses who miss a single interest payment after years of impeccable financial management.

Other small businesses resent those who do better
than themselves and develop a fine sense of superiority
over those who are below them, however slightly.

There is a vicious circle: no-one really trusts a small
business, so no-one gives it a chance, so it remains a
small business. To break the circle, everyone must
believe that it is:

- established longer than it really is,
- able to deliver a higher quality product than it really does,
- stronger financially than it really is,

and above all,

- bigger than it really is.

The Amateur Game

The first step in learning to bluff in business is to learn how to spot a bad bluffer. As with most things, there are two reasons for this:

1. Most of the people anyone in business will have to deal with are themselves in business. Although relatively few have studied the art of bluff, most are experienced enough to realise that their businesses depend upon it, and are quite capable of humiliating a would-be professional who underestimates them.

2. It is essential to learn how not to do it. The wise bluffer learns from the mistakes of others.

The amateur has grasped that is essential to pretend that one's business is more substantial than it actually is. Fortunately for the professional, the amateur always makes the same mistake: the **overbluff**.

The overbluff is best diagnosed as the condition of trying too hard to impress. Symptoms include:

a) shameless name-dropping.

b) drawing attention to expensive trappings – suit, car, office, etc. (Beware of lines like "Sorry, I left my mobile phone in my Gucci briefcase in the Jag.")

c) boasting about successful business deals, however trivial.

The last is the fatal mark of the amateur. Whenever you hear such boasting, you may draw two conclusions:

1. If one makes a big thing out of a little success it is a sign that such success is rare, and greater success is unknown. Boasting is a tell-tale sign of insecurity.

2. If one boasts whenever one has a success it follows that the absence of a boast is a clear indication of the absence of success, so a boaster who falls silent, even for a moment, is presumed dead.

Similarly, those who boast about how busy they are only make it obvious how unusual it is for them. In general, the harder one tries to impress the more obvious it is that one is desperate.

You should compare the boaster with the real thing, the truly successful entrepreneur. Indeed, before going into business you would do well to study the manner of those who have achieved what you aspire to.

A successful entrepreneur is so used to hard work, expensive possessions and meeting powerful people that they no longer seem worth talking about. He or she may enjoy so many successes that boasting becomes pointless, even tiresome. In fact, the wealthy entrepreneur will try to avoid attracting gold-diggers and time-wasters (the taxman and other entrepreneurs) and, being already established, will feel no need to impress anyone for commercial reasons.

Observe this and learn:

- not to refer to famous people ostentatiously by their first names.

  (The most effective way to name-drop is to use both Christian name and surname together, especially when talking of a peer or someone whose personal name is not generally used, in the middle of a list of more obscure names, made-up if necessary, in the same form and delivered in exactly the same tone. It implies you are no more impressed with the great one than you are by other personal acquaintances, or that you know other people who are just as important but whose importance is only appreciated by a select few, including yourself.)

- not to draw attention to your possessions. Those who are impressed with such things will have made a mental inventory before you can open your mouth, and they will be even more impressed if you appear to take it all for granted.

- not to mention business success. If the subject is raised, hint that your successes are too many and too commonplace to be discussed in detail.

You need to convey not merely that you are successful, but that you are successful and modest. The key is subtlety.

OBJECTIVES

The bluffer will not want to look like what he or she actually is, or even wants to be, but rather will wish to conform to the idea held by others of what a reliable business person looks like.

This varies from business to business; for example, someone in a traditional craft who tries to act like a business tycoon is asking to be derided, as does someone in a dynamic service industry who behaves like a country yokel.

You should study the norms of your chosen business and ask yourself:

- Is a premium placed on dynamism or reliability?

- Does your customer expect you to be aggressive or deferential? Loud or quiet? High tech or painstaking craftsman?

Don't try to be clever by doing the opposite to everyone else in the business. It can be a useful marketing gimmick, but usually the reason everyone behaves in a certain way is that they have found, over time, that the customer likes it that way.

It is up to you to investigate your chosen field, but most businesses will involve elements from the following basic models.

The Old School

Distinguishing features:

- socially secure: never worries about position, power, or (apparently) money

- impressed by absolutely nothing, and does not wish

to impress

- impeccably good manners at all times; not merely politeness, but genuine consideration for others.

Advantages:

- so hard to impress that others will go out of their way to try and impress you

- so obviously unconcerned about money that people will trust you with it. In general the best way to attract money is to appear not to want it; and the best way not to get something is to show that you really do want it

- so little need to impress that there is no need to spend a lot of money on expensive trappings, a great boon to the bluffer of limited resources.

Disadvantage:

Poor imitations are easily spotted. To carry it off successfully, one needs the proper training and practice (ideally a few years at Eton, then one of the more reactionary Oxford Colleges, followed by the Guards and/or the Foreign Office).

The Eternal Executive

Distinguishing features:

- talks in jargon, not English. (You will have no difficulty in making up jargon. Random groups of letters and numbers are particularly recommended: few people will be brave enough to admit their ignorance and ask what it all means.)

- takes great pains to appear very, very busy (to the extent of filling in diaries with fictitious appointments, arranging phone calls to interrupt meetings, and turning down any suggested date and time for a meeting to suggest an inconvenient hour instead).

- obsessed with expensive possessions, especially modern technology.

Advantage:

Easy for the bluffer with a bit of money. You don't need to be young, upwardly mobile, or professional either.

Disadvantage:

It doesn't really get you anywhere: this type has never quite realised how much everybody else despises them.

The Family Firm

Distinguishing features:

- appears old-established, and places great emphasis on tradition. Basic tasks such as letter writing or book keeping are performed in an unusual, even inefficient way that suggests 'it's the way grandfather did it so it's good enough for us'

- concerned with detail about everything, including quality of craftsmanship and finance. Invoices include comprehensive descriptions of the work done and the totals are never in round figures, but have a few odd pounds and pennies on the end – not £10,000 but £9,876.53

- absolutely classless.

Advantages:

– creates a marvellous air of reliability

– gives an excellent excuse for doing things economically. Family businesses, even the wealthiest, have always looked after their own, and their customers', pennies

– appeals to the creative bluffer who enjoys making up his or her own 'traditional' procedures.

Disadvantage:

Difficult to maintain if you're operating through a brand new off-the-shelf company.

The Honest Craftsman

Distinguishing features:

– looks the part: always wears appropriate work-clothes and a layer of appropriate dirt (but not the sort that offends) even when not working. People expect it.

– generally taciturn, except when talking about the job, when is prepared to talk with enthusiasm and in great detail.

Advantage:

Customers trust those they can pigeon-hole easily, especially if they feel socially superior, and will consider a craftsman who looks the part to be reliable.

Disadvantages:

– bluffers may find it hard to stomach pretending to be socially inferior to the customer

– of limited application (although **The Honest Professional** is similar in many respects, in which case your role model should be the traditional family solicitor).

The Eccentric

Distinguishing features:

– none (by definition).

Advantage:

– in certain businesses, when people see a real eccentric, they assume he or she must be very good indeed to act in such a fashion and still survive in business.

Disadvantage:

– you really do have to be eccentric to get away with it: if you're only slightly odd, people will think you're not quite all there and avoid you. To be acceptable, you have to be constantly outrageous – a 'real character', rather than just a cretin.

Whatever model you select, in general you must:

● Display total confidence, and try to appear relaxed at all times.

● Become familiar with the appropriate technical language.

● Be unafraid to appear mean at times. Remember that many millionaires are casual about large amounts but are prepared to haggle over a few pence. Perhaps that's why they are millionaires.

THE BUSINESS PLAN

Any **Business Plan** will probably be out of date before the final draft is typed. However well-researched it may be, it will never actually come to fruition. All the assumptions it makes will inevitably be flawed. The only things that are guaranteed to happen are those that could never be imagined (the First Law of Business Forecasting: expect the unexpected).

Yet it is absolutely essential that you have an up-to-date Business Plan. Inevitably there are two reasons for this:

1. It impresses would-be investors and bankers. The wildest predictions have a reassuring air of certainty about them when translated into Business School jargon, surrounded by columns of figures, laser printed, and placed in a shiny cover.

2. You must be consistent. If separate bluffs are not to contradict, it helps to have one's imaginary empire put down on paper. It also helps to refer to your Business Plan as often as possible in conversation. If you keep telling people that you're working to a plan, you might just give the impression that you know what you're doing.

A Business Plan should have three basic parts (each answering a separate question):

1. The **Mission Statement** ('Why am I doing this?')

2. The **Strategy** ('How am I doing this?')

3. The **Financial Data** ('What is this going to cost?')

Only the last one really matters, but it is important to pad it out with a full Plan containing as much surplus information as possible. It is possible, and desirable, to have more than the three basic sections (e.g. Human Resource Policies, etc.). A Business Plan must give the impression that every aspect has been thought out in excruciating detail.

1. The Mission Statement

The words 'Goals' or 'Purpose' are often used instead, and are probably more accurate, but the phrase 'Mission Statement' conveys a certain sense of destiny. It should define:

1. Exactly what business one is in. A short pithy sentence will do. It should be as broad as possible: a road haulage company should describe itself as being in the 'transport business', a printing company is in the 'communications business', and so on. It shows one takes it for granted that one is going to expand.

2. Why one is in it. This may seem obvious, so obvious that people never bother to think about it. In fact the majority of business people do not go into business with the sole aim of making large amounts of money. Research shows that:

   a) most would make more, certainly more per hour of work, if they were employed by someone else; and

   b) relatively few go into business with getting rich as the prime motive.

   People actually go into business for a wide variety of reasons including: the desire for independence and the ability to make their own decisions; the desire to do particular work or produce a particular product; the desire for a 'quiet' life outside the corporate rat-race; or any combination of motives, among them, of course, the desire for money.

It is vital that you sort out in your own mind exactly what you want out of business, because that should determine exactly how you operate. For example, an entrepreneur who wishes to get rich will adopt a high-risk strategy more heavily dependent on bluff, but someone who simply wants to earn a living doing work that he or she enjoys will be wise to adopt a low-risk strategy.

2. The Strategy

A good strategy should be as simple as possible.

Unfortunately such a strategy would hardly look impressive on paper. It must therefore be expanded with a number of superfluous sub-sections, such as:

Objectives

Not to be confused with 'goals' or 'purposes'. Where goals should be broad to the point of vagueness, objectives should be fairly precise: for example, a firm whose purpose is 'to build a global merchandising business' might have as objectives 'to take over the corner shop down the road' and 'to increase sales to £80,000 a year'.

One should be fairly consistent about maintaining one's objectives. The thing to avoid at all costs is the reputation of being a gadfly, flitting from one project to the next.

Market Profile

This is supposedly based on your 'Market Research'. However, formal market research is (a) expensive and (b) useless. The small business is more likely to rely on instinct and personal contacts – but, of course, you cannot actually say that. Instead, this is your chance to state at length what a marvellous business opportunity you have and how the world is crying out for whatever it is you are selling.

Economic Profile

Optional but a wonderful piece of padding in support of the Market Profile. Just get down to the nearest library and copy out some recent economic statistics – almost any statistics will do.

Trading Profile

This is where you show your expertise by showing you know how your chosen business is actually done: standard retail, wholesale, transport, credit arrangements, etc.

Competitor Profile

More easy padding. Details can usually be found in Trade publications. In more specialist businesses, where there are relatively few competitors, it might be worth copying out details of all of them from Companies House (if they are limited companies). It is also worthwhile getting your competitor's publicity material, especially price lists, and incorporating any hard information in the profile.

Customer Profile

Possibly separated into **corporate customers** and **consumers**. The former are fairly easy to describe (in terms of size and business), whilst the latter can be broken down by age, sex, and socio-economic grouping (using the magic letters A/B, C1, C2 and D/E: don't worry if you are not certain what the divisions represent; hardly anyone else does either).

Analysis

Real show-off stuff. There are hundreds of models for use in strategic analysis. Few of them are of any practical use outside Business Schools – most are too theoretical. You would do well just to hint that analysis has been carried out, without going into detail. If challenged, invent your own model (ideally something with a university name or a lot of letters in it: the Oxford Model or the CGT Model).

If you really must analyse something, use the 'SWOT Analysis' (by simply listing the internal Strengths and Weaknesses of your business, and the external Opportunities and Threats it faces in the market). Or the 'Benjamin Franklin Analysis' (even simpler – list the advantages and the disadvantages of any proposed course of action) also known, in a slightly different guise, as a 'Cost Benefit Analysis' or CBA.

Target Market

In reality, anyone who pays. But, once again, there is a difference between reality and what can be put in a Business Plan. You should be fairly specific, choosing one of the categories discussed in detail in the Customer Profile, but keeping your options open by mentioning 'valuable secondary markets'.

Marketing Plan

Small businesses can be divided into two categories: those dependent on large numbers of sales of small value, and those dependent on small numbers of sales of larger value. In the former case, there is an established way of contacting customers (such as passing trade for a small corner shop), whilst the latter will probably rely on personal contacts.

Since you can hardly say that your Marketing Plan depends on your "brother-in-law who is head of purchasing for a major company", you should discuss your 'Marketing Mix', a useful expression meaning the combination of traditional marketing methods such as advertising, direct sales, mailing, promotions – including 'POS' (point of sale), etc. Even if such methods are entirely inappropriate, they are worth mentioning to show you are aware of them.

Competitive Advantage

Also known as 'USP' (Unique Selling Proposition). Conventional Business School wisdom has it that there are two ways of distinguishing yourself from the competition: 'Price Differentiation '(being cheaper) or 'Product Differentiation' (being better, or at least different). The bluffer's real competitive advantage is of course the ability to bluff, but since that is one of the many truths one cannot actually put in writing, the best USP is probably a nebulous Product Differentiation like 'superior quality of service'.

Sales Forecast

Very important, but best avoided because someone might hold you to it. Be vague, or at least qualify it as much as possible ('assuming an increased rate of economic growth', etc.).

Operations Plan

A slightly more impressive way of saying 'Production Plan'. Most people produce something first and worry about selling it afterwards. The far-sighted will do it the other way round – worry about delivery once you know you will get paid for it.

Policies

The final touch. Policy, in general, is the framework within which a business operates. The most important policies are the strategic objectives themselves, but even the smallest firm might have a range of additional policies from major moral constraints to standard administrative procedures. (Policies are in turn subject to 'doctrine', a word which is sometimes used to describe the more rigid policies.)

A comprehensive list of corporate doctrines and policies in a Business Plan would look a little too obvious, but a short note showing you are aware of the need and explaining your procedure for formulating them (e.g. 'Policy will be set by the Board on the recommendation of the Chief Executive') might be acceptable.

Summary of The Strategy

A summary of the strategy is an excuse to bring in your real strategy under the guise of a short synopsis.

In general, a good strategy should include:

1. As many figures as possible. (Don't worry about their accuracy or relevance – no-one will actually read them, but they will be reassured to see them there.)

2. As many long, American-sounding words and phrases as possible. (As a rule, prefix everything with 'long-term' or 'short-term' or 'medium-term', and end it with 'ization'. And never use two syllables where five or six would be more confusing, or one word where three would take more space. Never be afraid of making up your own business expressions: there are so many that no reader will know them all and will be unwilling to state positively that yours are not in general use somewhere.)

3. As many repetitions (or, at least rephrasings) of your basic points as you can fit in without becoming obvious.

It is a nice touch to number pages, headings, sub-headings, sections, sub-sections, paragraphs, and sub-paragraphs, using a consistent system. You can then cross-reference ('as discussed in 3.9.14.8' or, in the more archaic style, 'see sub-paragraph 1(4) (c) (ii), in chapter 2, part II, p.37'). This looks good and makes it less likely that it will be read in any detail (only the most dedicated masochist will try checking cross-references). Keep paragraphs short, but make sure there are plenty of them.

Remember that it is unlikely that anyone will read your strategy with any great attention, especially if you make it as long as you can. Anyone who has any real interest in the Business Plan will home in on the Financial Data without hesitation. However, it is essential that the Strategy which precedes it – and on which the financial data are supposed to be based – looks right to the casual eye.

3. The Financial Data

These form the most important part of any Business Plan, because, unlike the rest of it, they will be read. More than that, they will probably be read in great detail by clever people seeking to prove their cleverness by catching you out on some tiny point of detail which could undermine the credibility of the whole Plan.

As far as a small business is concerned, there are four types of financial data:

1. **Budgets** – what you hope will happen.

2. **Forecasts** – what you think will happen.

3. **Outturn** – what actually does happen.

4. **Accounts** – what your Accountant says has happened.

The Business Plan must include a **Budget**. When it becomes clear that this is completely unrealistic, it can be updated by **Forecasts**, which in turn can be replaced by '**Revised Forecasts**' when they, too, prove to be inaccurate.

It is absolutely vital that you are always able to point to an up-to-date plan which shows that the finances are on target (even if that plan was only produced the night before to formalise an existing situation). It gives bankers and investors the reassuring illusion that you are in control.

It might be a good idea to blur the distinction between Budget and Forecast by using that all-encompassing word '**Estimates**' to replace both.

The proper format for a Budget is a matter of endless debate, but you would do well to forget any idea of trying to draw up model Balance Sheets, and Profit and Loss Accounts, based on what you think your Accountant will draw up at the end of the first year. There are naturally two reasons for this:

1. It is meaningless: everyone knows that such formal accounts bear little relationship to reality; one would change accountants if they did.

2. It is fiendishly difficult to do. You really need to be an accountant to do it properly, and even then any reader with the slightest training in financial management can, and will, pick holes in it. Even if it is done by an accountant you can never be sure that the reader will not be used to a different system, and if you yourself were to be examined in detail it could be very awkward indeed.

As with most things, it is best to keep it simple. A **Cash Flow Analysis**, whilst frowned on by purists, is:
   a) easier to do,
   b) more impressive because it involves putting far more figures on the page, and
   c) actually rather useful because it shows you how many real pounds and pennies go in and out rather than how many notional ones.

A Cash Flow Analysis is drafted as follows:

1. Write the 12 months of the year across the top of your page (if there is no room for the full name just use the first three letters), starting with the month that begins your financial year, leaving broad spaces on either side for the financial year in the top left hand corner and the word 'Total' in the top right hand corner.

2. Down the left hand side, list all categories of income, then all the categories of expenditure, leaving a line for 'Total' and a space below both, and adding another line at the very bottom, the proverbial Bottom Line, for 'Surplus/(Deficit)', i.e. Total Income minus Total Expenditure.

3. Fill in credible sums for each category for each month, then calculate and record in the appropriate columns:

- the annual **Total** for each category

- the total **Income and Expenditure** for each month and for the entire year

- the monthly and annual **Surplus** (or **Deficit**).

It is a good idea to have as few categories of **Income** as possible: in business you find that sales you expect, and rely on, never emerge, but money sometimes comes out of the blue from a direction you never envisaged. By not being specific about sources of income your reputation as a business prophet will not be damaged. It is essential that others believe you have the ability to predict what will happen to your business, however illogical that may be.

On the other hand, **Expenditure** should be divided into as many categories as possible. The more you have, the greater the number of figures you can stick on a page and the more you can show your mastery of detail.

However imaginative you may be, there will inevitably be items of expenditure that you miss out. Some will be fairly obvious: cost of sales (e.g. raw materials), rent, rates, gas, electricity, telephone, insurance, etc. Yet those who remember interest payments often forget about bank charges and arrangement fees, or put down wages and associated costs (e.g. national insurance) for their employees, but not for themselves.

Then there are the so-called 'variable costs' which are supposed to vary according to one's level of business, but don't. These include advertising, publicity and other promotional material, travel and entertainment, and most other marketing costs.

There are also all the minor expenses one never really thinks of in advance but which have to be paid if the business is to operate. For example:

- stationery;

- postage;

- professional fees (especially accountants');

- company administration (such as the fee paid to Companies House every year);

- office furniture, office fittings, office refreshments (i.e. coffee);

- office equipment (not only the photocopier, the word processor and the dictaphone, but the toner, data discs, and the tapes one needs to use them);

- 'office supplies', the safety-net category of everything from light bulbs, coffee cups, lavatory paper, pencil sharpeners, the Office Ruler, cleaning and security equipment, and spare keys, to miscellaneous batteries.

Of course, the more categories one has, the greater the chances that at least one will go drastically and noticeably over budget.

Two precautions can be taken against this:

1. Have several categories which are fairly broad and vague so that if one is overspent it will be possible to transfer to another category certain items which could reasonably be found in either: for example, a coffee machine could be classed under 'office furniture', 'office fittings', 'office equipment', 'office refreshments', or the ubiquitous 'office supplies'.

2. Put a very large sum under **'Contingencies'**. You will probably need it. Even if you don't, anyone who knows business will respect your caution and foresight in being prepared.

Despite these precautions, it is still quite probable that your expenditure Estimates will prove inaccurate. Expenditure which is substantially below budget can be put down to 'savings due to good management practice'. But so can expenditure which is above that predicted in the Budget – such as:

'An opportunity arose to buy capital equipment which will drastically reduce our running costs over the next few years'

'We found that employing an extra clerk will reduce the workload of existing sales staff and enable them to increase their revenues by far more than the cost of the new employee'

'This new marketing initiative will finance itself through increased sales'

and, best of all,

'The unexpectedly large public response to our promotion has meant additional expenditure to enable us to cope with enquiries.'

Try to make your Estimates as realistic as possible. Make an effort to think of the thousands of things which might cost money. You won't be able to think of them all, but the more you can predict in advance, the smaller the chance of an unexpected bill cropping up just when you don't want it.

Obtain quotes in advance where possible, as well as information about fixed costs (e.g. standing charges, statutory fees) and put them in your Estimates correct to the nearest pound, not rounded up. It looks very impressive to have a few odd pounds on the page, and shows that you have done your research.

The amateur bluffer might try to fool bankers and investors with over-optimistic profits, but such figures always reveal themselves as the hype that they are.

It is better to be cautious, to predict modest but acceptable profits whilst leaving room for a considerable margin of error.

Draw up a first draft on the basis of the most realistic figures you can get, and then:

- **halve** your sales forecasts

- **double** your costs

- **double** the amount of time your customers take to pay.

This way any informed reader will realise that you know about small business.

Playing with Models

Having drawn up your basic Estimates, you might want to play around with them. With a computer or word processor you can create as many different variations as you want. For example:

1. More than one 'model' on the basis of different growth forecasts. Using the same format, you can show three different sets of Estimates, one 'optimistic', one 'pessimistic', and one 'probable' – the last being the real one.

2. Detailed Estimates not only for your first year in business, but the next three, or even five, years (although the word 'Forecast' should be used to describe Estimates beyond the first year to distinguish them from the supposedly firmer figures for that year, despite the fact that the fifth year figures will probably not be much more accurate than the first).

   You can either add a fixed percentage to all figures in subsequent years to cover inflation (10 per cent is a good figure as it is best to be pessimistic with inflation and it is an easy figure to work with), or state that all figures are at current-year price. Once again, different models using different growth assumptions can be produced for each year.

The object, of course, is to create a visually impressive wedge of paper covered in figures which should daunt the most compulsive critic. Even with a single year's Estimates and no additional models, it may not be possible to fit everything into a single page. Spreadsheets may be used, but might give your Business Plan an untidy, bulky look.

3. An alternative might be to put a one-page summary on the first page of your Estimates, and then break it down by note, i.e. after each category put a number in brackets, the number being that of a subsequent page where that category is broken down into sub-categories using the same format.

The sub-categories can, in turn, be broken down by notes for a really thick document. This is an old accountants' trick to increase the thickness of your accounts and the size of their fees.

Finally, the Financial Data, indeed the whole Business Plan, should always be kept up to date through constant **Reviews** in which discredited Estimates are replaced.

If, by some miracle, your Estimates prove accurate, insert a '**Variance**' column which shows the difference, or rather the lack of difference, between Estimate and Outturn.

Whatever you may be doing at any time, it helps to be able to point to a piece of paper which says you are supposed to be doing it.

STARTING UP

To Be or Not To Be (Incorporated)

Before you even decide on the name of your business, you have to think about whether you want any letters after it and, if so, which (Ltd., PLC, Inc., Pty., SA, etc.).

There are legal and financial arguments both for and against incorporation. The decisive factor will probably be your tax position.

From a bluffer's point of view, incorporation is desirable because it brings with it two big advantages:

1. **A separate legal identity** (which should, in itself, appeal to you, since your object after all is to appear to be a completely different person)

2. **Limited liability**.

If there was any logic in the world both these features ought to make people more suspicious when doing business with limited companies.

Yet it seems that many people and, strangest of all, many companies, find it reassuring to deal with a limited company. Those who would never accept a small cheque without a bankers' card and proof of identity will often accept a large cheque drawn on a limited company without hesitation.

Perhaps their confidence is based on the statutory regulation of limited companies or on their own ability to check a company's details at Companies House should they so choose. Few do, but it is sensible to search any company you are doing a substantial amount of business with, especially if any form of credit is involved. More likely, most people (against all evidence) have a mental image of a 'company' as a large, established, reliable organisation like General Motors. Those who own small companies ought to know better, but perhaps they feel obliged to take an exalted view of companies in general in order to protect their own positions.

Who's Who

It is tempting as head of a small business to become 'Company Director'. But the bluffer ought to have a more specific title to imply being part of a larger organisation, such as 'Executive Director', 'Administrative Director', or 'Company Secretary' (a statutory post usually held by a specialist in a large company, but often held by the director who runs the whole show in a small one).

Some who start out in business give themselves titles like Chairman, President, Managing Director and Chief Executive Officer of their company, and so reveal themselves as people who are unfamiliar with companies. Such megalomania would be very dangerous in a big public limited company with suspicious shareholders and keen office politicians fighting each other for every scrap of status.

It is far more effective, and far closer to modern practice, not to have a large number of impressive-sounding posts at the top in order to show a lean, efficient management structure, and for such posts as there are to be filled by different people. There are sound theoretical reasons why the posts of Chairman and Managing Director should be separate in a big business; in a small business there is the added advantage of showing that the company has more than one executive.

It is highly necessary to pretend that you are not, in fact, the top person in the company. This might go against the grain, but there are two definite advantages:

1. Employees have a better reputation than entrepreneurs. Anyone can be an entrepreneur and can flit from one business to the next without having to make a long-term commitment to any one of them. On the other hand, it is assumed that employees are carefully screened and selected, and that they will wish to develop long-term careers with the company so will be careful not to endanger that. It is also reassuring if someone is supervised by, and answerable to, some form of higher authority.

2. If you are answerable to someone else it is only natural that the mental picture others form of your unseen superior is that of a person who must be, in every way, more impressive than yourself. This may help them to overlook any shortcomings you might have in the same way that you might show a little more respect to an unimpressive clerk if he represents Lord Hanson. It is even more reassuring to outsiders if you are perceived as being answerable not just to one person, but to several – especially if they take the form of an official body such as a formal Board of Directors.

It is therefore a good idea to provide the company with a nominal Chairman of the Board, ideally with a different surname (unless pursuing the strategy of pretending to be a family firm).

It is even more imposing if one can afford several **Non-Executive Directors**. Having a proper Board adds a great deal of dignity to a small company, and so gives it a more reliable image.

The sort of person who makes a good Non-Executive will probably have done the job before and will know what is expected (i.e. to keep quiet and let you get on with running the company in return for a small fee for

33

turning up at the occasional meeting). Most Non-Executives are also good sources of information and business contacts, and can prove to be a very useful resource. There is no shortage of people willing to serve as Non-Executives (and most are cheaper than one might imagine). Good raw material includes:

Peers

By no means all are rich, and many would welcome any sort of regular cash income. It might be worth a look at Burke's or Debrett's, especially for those who enjoy only a courtesy title, with no privileges or estates attached, as the eldest sons of high-ranking peers who are still alive, and for Scottish and Irish peers who have the titles but no seats in the House of Lords.

MPs

Most MPs are obscure back-benchers without the fabled portfolios of directorships and consultancies; some would be grateful for an additional source of income, however small, especially since their main profession gives them little job security.

Local Worthies

(Especially those with letters after their names.) People who spend a great deal of their time in one sort of public service or another have less time to make money for themselves.

Other Entrepreneurs

Those who are either 'consulting' (the nearest any entrepreneur will ever be to retired) and those who desire a little part-time work in addition to their full-time job with their own business, in order to diversify their business interests, probably make the most useful Non-Executives. Also the most dangerous. A really good one is quite capable of taking over your business.

It may cost a little to put a good Board together, but it will be worth it. You will not just be selling

E. N. Trepreneur, Proprietor

but

Directors: Lord Inverapenny (Chairman)
Sir A. Back-Bencher MP
Councillor L. O. Calworthy OBE JP DL
E.N. Trepreneur (Secretary)

It doesn't matter if no-one has heard of your Non-Executive Directors. In business there is an assumption that obscurity means you are too powerful to feel the need to publicise yourself. Having a celebrity on the Board can create entirely the wrong image. On the other hand, never invent fictitious directors – it is too easy to check.

Building an Empire

The only thing more impressive than a limited company is a **Group of Companies**. You would do well to create as many companies as you can afford, and to organise at least some of them into a coherent Group. (Others ought to be kept at arm's length from the Group as a sort of commercial escape hatch.)

The words 'Group of Companies' tend to lend an image of a large, established organisation. So do the words 'Public Limited Company'. It is, in fact, not much more difficult to create a PLC than it is to set up a private limited company: there is no obligation to sell shares to the general public, or to put it on the Stock Exchange. You could easily make the 'flagship' of the Group a PLC.

The only problem with all these companies is the obligation to file annual details which will enable an interested party, probably the person you most want to impress, to find out exactly how small you really are.

The solution is to keep moving. You have more than a year before you are obliged to file the first returns of a new company, so if you keep setting up new companies, and taking your business through them, it will be very difficult for anyone to draw an up-to-date picture of your operations.

At the same time it will be necessary to keep at least one old-established company as the flagship of the Group if you are to avoid the reputation of operating through fly-by-night companies. You could buy an existing company, provided it is clear of liabilities. The old company is the one which attracts the business and makes the initial contact, but it can then turn the customer over to a new company which does the actual work. Make sure the customer knows exactly which company he or she is dealing with or you could get into fearsome legal difficulties.

The final touch is to add a couple of foreign companies to your Group, especially those registered in noted offshore tax havens. Once again, this should make people more suspicious of you. After all, you can hide information and assets outside the jurisdiction of the British legal system. Yet many see such companies as evidence that you are:

a) big, multi-national, and therefore more reliable.
b) on the ball when it comes to financial management.

The added advantage is that operating through a

36

foreign company relieves one of the obligation to make company details public, and invests your company with an enjoyable air of mystery.

In this way every company of the Group, no matter how insignificant, can have its own separate bankers and team of professional advisers. It is possible to create a complex legal network, involving the proverbial paper trail of companies and bank accounts, and a large number of individuals – advisers, partners, agents, etc., some of them quite powerful – each of whom knows just a little bit about one's affairs, but has no idea how big (or small) the whole thing really is.

What's in a Name?

Never underestimate the importance of a company's name. It is the first thing the customer comes into contact with. Not the least of your considerations should be your place in the telephone directory: there are obvious advantages in a name like 'Aardvark Industries Limited' but 'AA Limited' might give quite the wrong impression.

You should not consider trading under the random set of letters and/or numbers that come with an off-the-shelf company. To do so is not merely a wasted opportunity, but a symptom of laziness and lack of imagination.

Company names based on letters or numbers might seem dynamic at first, but that soon wears off. They tend to be associated with the sort of entrepreneur whose companies don't last very long. They can also seem impersonal, unless based on a longer name which has been shortened over the years not by the company itself so much as by popular usage (ICI, BT, AT&T), which only tends to happen with large and illustrious organisations.

If you wish to stress reliability, rather than dynamism and originality, it is better to use a name that includes a description of the type of business and/or the geographical area in which you operate. The implication is that you are established in that business or area, committed to it, and proud of it.

The drawback with such names is that they can prove restrictive if you ever diversify or expand. However, many large companies retain names based on products or areas that have long ceased to provide them with their main sources of income, because such names suggest tradition and continuity. The bluffer who tries to simulate this would do well to think of a name which sounds as specialised, as localised and, ideally, as archaic as possible, so that no-one could ever imagine it being confined to the trade and/or locality given in the name (like 'Old Sarum Saddlers Co. Ltd.').

Yet the most reliable companies are those with a personal or family name on their letterheads. There is no greater outward symbol of commitment to a company than a willingness to put one's own name on it. The mental images associated with such names are of old-established family firms, including banks, professional partnerships, and businesses with strong local traditions.

If you have adopted the wise course of pretending that you are not the company, but merely a small, if significant, cog in a larger corporate machine, it is a good idea to name the company after someone else (and install a nominal Chairman with at least one of the names found on the letterhead).

If, on the other hand, you do not wish to hide the fact that you are in control, you might as well go the whole hog and complete the image of a strong personality by naming the company after yourself. There is a general assumption that no-one would want to dishonour a company which bears one's own name – an assumption made by people who do not know it is quite easy to transfer the name to another company in the event of an emergency. A problem only occurs if you sell the entire business to someone else, and would have liked to use your own name again for the next one.

The Imperial Style

If you have invested in a Group of Companies, the names of most of the subsidiaries should be slight variations on the name of the flagship company, the one with your name on. The slight differences may reflect the different specialist types of business, the areas in which they operate, or the places where they are registered. Thus the subsidiaries of 'John Smith Ltd.' might include:

John Smith (Transport) Ltd.
John Smith (Property) Ltd.
John Smith (North West) Ltd.
John Smith (Jersey) Ltd.
John Smith (Luxembourg) S.A.

At the same time, it might be a good idea to have within the Group companies with completely different names, implying that you have taken over someone else's company or that you are engaged in a joint venture with another business, in order to suggest that not all of your eggs are in one basket.

Other Options

It is still possible to trade under a number of business names, with no obligation to submit any information to Companies House. One option might be to create a network of nominal or fictional partnerships. These can, in many ways, operate like limited companies: you can use the title 'Senior Partner' instead of Chairman, and 'Managing Partner' instead of Managing Director.

Since most other types of business are usually incorporated, partnership is now associated mainly with those professional advisers whose governing bodies discourage or forbid incorporation.

Alternatively you can operate in the 'Trading as' mode – which at least has the advantage of no formal (i.e. expensive) accounts.

Creating an Image

First impressions last. If your business starts off by making a bad impression – or even worse, by making no impression at all – it will take years to correct, if it can be corrected. Most small businesses do not have years to spare.

Some people might be tempted to hedge their bets, to hold resources back from the launch of a business in case it becomes necessary to pay for a relaunch. Such people do not belong in business.

The true entrepreneur must be prepared to bet everything on his or her judgement. In any case, it is difficult enough for a small business to make a big enough splash to be noticed, even with all its available resources. If those resources are divided in order to pay for a series of tiny ripples, instead of the big splash, it is even more unlikely that the business will make any sort of impression. Moreover, any relaunch will inevitably be more difficult to carry off than the original launch because it will have to cost at least as much as the one that failed and, in fear of further failure, probably more.

Most small businesses are not noted for having large piles of spare cash lying around, so what money there is has to be spent effectively. The bright bluffer will spend it where it can be seen.

High Quality Headed Paper

In most businesses the first thing a customer will see of your company will not be you, your staff or your premises, but your letterhead.

The successful business will use heavy, high quality paper (100 gsm or more). Have as much information as possible without the page becoming cluttered. If you have invested in a limited company or group of companies, a full Board of Non-Executive Directors and any number of phone and fax lines, put it all on your note-paper. But avoid the additional expense of matching envelopes. The odds are that they will be thrown away by secretaries long before the letters they contain reach the desks of the people they are intended to impress.

Business Cards

In contrast to the letterhead, your name on your business card should be as discreet as possible. Business cards – indeed, all promotional material – should follow the same **corporate identity**. Having a corporate identity simply means making sure all material put out by your business has the same logo, layout and lettering. It makes it easier for everyone (including yourself) to remember which company you are.

A Good Word Processor and Printer

It is pointless having the most beautiful paper in the world if it is covered in inferior type or print. A business that sends out a great many letters should invest in the best computer and printer it can afford.

A Prestigious Address
(without the expense of having to be there)

It is not necessary to rent an outrageously priced office in a fashionable area when all one wants is the address. It is fairly easy to obtain a convenience address; the advanced bluffer might want to have more than one (e.g. New York, Tokyo, the Solomon Islands – any place where it might be deemed advantageous for your particular business). Anyone wanting to meet you personally will be just as happy meeting at their own place or on neutral ground, such as a restaurant.

It is also possible to use someone else's telephone number (perhaps with an answering service), fax or even web site. One might not even have to pay, if one has obliging friends who already have these facilities.

An Experienced P.A.*

A good personal assistant is more than a labour-saving device and status symbol. The fact that you are an employer, even if you only have one employee, rather than a lone wolf, will gain you standing straight away.

A good P.A. will be your partner in bluff: it is not easy to believe something when only one person says it, but it becomes more credible when two people appear to believe it.

*The ancient and honourable title of Secretary ('one responsible for secrets') has been supplanted by the strange designation of Personal Assistant which seems to be preferred by the actual practitioners, though there was never any suggestion of the US Personal Assistant of State negotiating with the General Personal Assistant of the Soviet Communist Party in the good old days.

MARKETING

The point of any business is to persuade someone else to give you money (traditionally in return for some product or service, but that's not the important bit).

Marketing is simply the word bluffers have coined to describe the grubby business of 'selling'. The bluffer will never admit this. Indeed, the word 'selling' should never pass your lips, and even 'marketing' should not be used in mixed company (i.e. in front of prospective customers or clients). So if:

Marketing = Selling, and
Selling = Business, and
Business = Bluff

logic dictates that

Marketing = Bluff.

However, you should never be caught bluffing when selling because:

1. If a sale is found to be based on selective information, it could be void at law. The buyer could claim his or her money back, and the seller could be liable to civil, or even criminal, action. Even if one escapes the just consequences of one's action...

2. It's unsporting.

When marketing, you are a sportsman engaged on the greatest hunt of all. As with any hunt there are rules, and there is a proper order in which things are done. First of all, one must identify one's prey; then one comes into contact with it; and only then can one bring it home. Thus:

1. **Market Research** – identifies the customer.

2. **Promotion** – makes contact with the customer.

3. **Distribution** – delivers the product or service.

1. Market Research

In the popular mind 'market research' consists of someone with a clipboard asking people in the street what they think of a particular product or service.

However the bluffer will view it as a far broader process, involving the formulation of strategy, new product development, test marketing, and the gathering of a great deal of information of which consumer canvassing (i.e. clipboards) is a relatively minor part.

There are two reasons why you should adopt this broad approach:

1. It provides a good excuse for not having done the narrow clipboard-bearing sort of 'market research' which for most small businesses is too expensive, and may be superfluous if the business does not deal with a mass market.

2. It allows you to work out exactly who your customer is, and how he or she is best approached. A business dealing with a small number of relatively high-spending customers ought to have a completely different marketing strategy from one with a large number of relatively low spenders.

Only when you are sure where your customers can be found should you start trying to attract their attention.

2. Promotion

Promotion includes anything that might attract the customer's weary eyes towards your product. This covers a wide variety of sins from POS displays to alleged 'Competitions', 'Special offers', and 'Sales' that go on forever.

Advertising

The small business can forget about mass media campaigns: to penetrate the collective consciousness and establish your product as a 'brand' name is far too expensive (and cannot be guaranteed). Advertising is pointless unless you are prepared to do it properly which means spending more money than most small businesses are ever likely to see.

However, in most businesses there is a trade paper or magazine which is traditionally read with attention by everyone connected with that business, including anyone interested in its product or service. A relatively small ad there could be all that is needed.

Nor should you neglect classified telephone directories, or trade directories – the main sources of information for people looking for a product or service who do not have a current supplier or contact. Such people tend to assume that the most established and reliable firm will be the one with the biggest advertisement. Don't disappoint them.

Then there is the classified ads section of a local paper, where even the biggest advertisement need not be very big. You can always justify your low level of advertising expenditure by claiming that your produce is fairly exclusive and that you are appealing to a particular 'niche' in the market.

Press and Public Relations

This should appeal to the subtle bluffer who enjoys the idea of marketing by pretending not to market.

By using the editorial, rather than the classified pages of a newspaper, you can promote your business without the cost of actually paying for advertising.

The most obvious method is to donate some money to charity: it needn't be much to get your photograph in the local paper, handing a cheque to a local worthy.

Charitable donations create an image of a business that is:

a) big and profitable (it must be if it has money to give away), and

b) the sort of business one does not mind giving one's money to (in the vague belief that some of it will be passed on to a good cause).

Major decision-makers, or members of their immediate families, are often involved with charitable, social, arts, sports, educational, environmental, political or other local organisations for whom a couple of hundred pounds is a lot of money. A small business will not be able to sponsor a performance at Covent Garden, but an advertisement in the programme for a village fête might be seen (and actually read) by more high-spenders than any glossy brochure sent to their offices. In their spare time, even the great notice little things.

The bluffer should also cultivate politicians. They are usually eager to help and can be useful, attracting mutual publicity by opening factories, serving as Non-Executive Directors, smoothing the way when dealing with bureaucrats, etc.

And don't forget journalists. Contrary to legend,

few journalists can be bribed with drink, but good social relations help to keep channels of communication open. So do regular briefings (especially if spiced with some good gossip, whether on or off the record) in addition to putting absolutely anything that might give your business publicity into a press release.

The Press release should not err on the side of modesty:

COMPANY EXPANDS: NEW JOBS ON THE WAY
(New cleaner taken on.)

EXECUTIVE TEAM STRENGTHENED
(New clerk taken on.)

JOBS AT RISK
(The standard line when a public authority threatens to do something the company doesn't like.)

LOCAL FIRM IN TALKS WITH U.S. GIANT
(They phoned to ask about the price.)

LOCAL FIRM SIGNS CONTRACT WITH U.S. GIANT
(We actually sold them something.)

U.S GIANT AND LOCAL FIRM LINK UP
(They gave us a local sales agency.)

U.S. GIANT AND LOCAL FIRM IN PARTNERSHIP DEAL
(The sales agency is a joint-venture: we split the profits.)

LOCAL FIRM TO TAKE OVER U.S. GIANT?
(Well, anyone can speculate, can't they?)

Telephone Canvassing

This has one big advantage: the customer cannot see you and therefore does not know how small your business really is.

Direct Mailing

The bluffer's best hope. A letter is impersonal: the recipient does not know if it is from a big business or a desperate one.

It is possible to buy a good mailing list suited to your business needs – a good investment if you can afford it – but it might be too expensive. If so, you can create your own using trade directories, classified telephone directories, local business directories, electoral rolls, and so on.

If you do not have the name and exact title of the addressee, use the most prestigious title you can imagine each functionary having, e.g. if you are selling office supplies, 'The Director of Administration'. When in doubt, go straight to the top and write to 'The Chief Executive', the form of address most likely to get your letter to the real power, whatever his or her true title.

Having gone to all that trouble one should get as much use as possible out of one's mailing list: there is no harm in mailing the same people again and again.

Eventually they might begin to take you seriously.

Direct Sales

In many businesses, especially those whose customers are other businesses, a great deal is done through social contact. Turning a non-business contact into a business contact is a skill that can be learnt only by experience. It helps if an entrepreneur gets around as much as possible and becomes involved in organisations to which prospective customers belong. Join as many as your resources permit.

Do not imagine that fellow members will suddenly provide you with business just because you are one of them, but if you make them aware of your business the day may come when you might be given the chance to put in a competitive quote simply because they happen to know you personally. Always have your business cards ready.

3. Distribution

Think of distribution not as part of the selling process, but as a continuation of the process of promotion.

The packaging, the company name on the delivery van, the physical presence of the product itself – all are forms of advertising.

Delivery should always be accompanied by a fanfare, even in businesses without a product in the traditional sense: a construction firm will put a large sign outside a building it is repairing; an accountant will usually deliver accounts in a binder with the firm's name on it; and a lawyer will put on fancy dress.

OPERATIONS

Having gone to all that trouble to sell a product or service, it seems rather unfair that you have to provide it as well. Unfortunately, most customers tend to insist on getting something in return for their money, unreasonable cads that they are.

So the question is 'What product?' To which the true entrepreneur will reply 'Anything I can sell.' Nevertheless, you ought to have a main or principal product of some sort. It provides you with a ready answer to the question 'What business are you in?'

An evasive reply will make everyone assume you must be into something shady. As an entrepreneur you will have enough trouble trying to establish a reliable reputation without people thinking that you must be a gun runner.

When selecting your principal product, consider the extent to which it can be used as the base for a broader range of products. Where possible, subsidiary companies should be set up to handle each of those sidelines so that if one of the sidelines turns sour the main business is not damaged.

Having selected a product, your next question is how to produce it. The answer is: you don't. As a rule a small business should never actually produce a product.

Production costs money: selling makes money.

Production is a pain. It takes up time (better spent selling) and money (spent on plant, machinery and labour). Even if you reduce your costs through vigorous self-denial and constant vigilance you are unlikely to be able to match the low unit costs, or quality, of mass production and economies of scale*.

* 'Economies of scale' is business school speak for 'Big is Beautiful'.

The answer is to sell something produced by someone else. Either:

- Obtain agencies to sell the products of another company, or,

- Employ producers to do your production for you on a sub-contract basis.

There are thousands of variations on the above, most notably the mutual reference arrangement which means that both you and your producer act as agents for each other. In general, you cannot have too many business contacts, however casual, whether they are prepared to pay you commission to sell their products, prepared to sell your products in return for commission, or willing to produce for you at need.

It is worth remembering that the word 'entrepreneur', loosely translated, is French for 'middleman'.

DEALING WITH PEOPLE

The Bank Manager

The Bank Manager is the most powerful person in the world of small business.

If you already have money, the Bank Manager will be only too eager to lend money to you. But if you already have money, you wouldn't be bothering with small business.

The bluffer will immediately grasp that the key to the situation is convincing the Bank Manager that one has heaps of money, and doesn't really need to borrow more, but would like to do so anyway. There are of course, two slight problems with this:

a) Any sensible person (and bank managers are always the most sensible of people) will wonder why you want to borrow money if you say you already have enough.

b) Your Bank Manager has a better idea of how much money you have than you do.

So trying to bluff a Bank Manager is a bit like trying to out-eat a Sumo wrestler: it is theoretically possible but just not very likely.

But there are steps you can take which will put you at less of a disadvantage:

1. Think big

The same Bank which sends you letters if you are a few pence over your overdraft limit seems to be more than happy to lend millions to some of the most dubious businessmen in the world. This is because banks assume that someone who asks for

£100,000 is used to dealing with such sums and is not worried about paying it back, while someone who asks for £100 is obviously a small time loser. It pays to over-estimate your needs.

The Bank Manager will wish to demonstrate his control by giving you less than you ask for. So if you want £10,000, ask for £30,000. (He will halve the sum, but you will inevitably find that you need half as much again as you thought you did.)

2. Exploit your Business Plan

The figures in your Plan should support your position that you are doing very nicely and expect to be doing even better as a result of the business, but can foresee times when you might, under certain circumstances, have temporary cash flow difficulties. You want a secure credit facility just in case. Bank Managers adore cautious people.

3. Increase your credit rating over time

Borrow money when you don't need it in order to demonstrate your ability to pay it back. Having proved your ability with small loans, gradually increase their size. Your record will not save you if things go bad, but a large loan facility may help to keep your options open.

4. Create the illusion of cash flow

It helps to have accounts with several banks (which increasingly means using several businesses) and several accounts with each bank (e.g. one deposit, one current, one for wages or money held on trust for customers). Such money as one has should be put into a pool which moves from one account to another.

It should not be too obvious: whilst the income of each account should look regular and reliable, expenditure should be more erratic. Ideally, at the end of a series of transfers there should be a little more left in each account than there was at the start: the important thing is to give an impression of high volume of turnover so that the Bank Manager believes your loan is but a small percentage of your total income.

5. Avoid offering imaginary collateral

Try to build up your credit rating without offering collateral or security of any sort because you not only want to get money out of the bank, you want to avoid having to repay it at an inconvenient moment – i.e. when you don't have it. If the bank has more to lose than you by foreclosing, it might, just might, give you a bit more time*.

The Accountant

A good Accountant can be defined as one who saves you in taxes almost as much as he charges in fees.

Most entrepreneurs treat their Accountants as their Father Confessor – friend, guide and Fount of All Wisdom. This is a mistake. Accountants will always err on the side of caution in order to protect themselves with the taxman.

* But probably won't.

Once again, it is an advantage to operate through as many different businesses as possible. Each should have its own accountant, with yet another accountant looking after your own personal finances. No bluffer will allow anyone to know everything about his or her affairs.

The same applies to all professional advisers, solicitors, brokers, consultants, architects, surveyors, engineers... And always remember that every supplier, including the professional adviser, is also a potential customer, and one cannot have too many of those.

The Personal Assistant

You might, if you're very good, bluff your banker, your accountant, even your family, but you will never bluff your P.A. Nor should you try. He or she must be your ally in carrying off your bluff.

All contact must be made through your P.A. You must be unavailable much of the time, even if you're not actually doing anything. This will mean much more work for you since, for example, you will have to return the calls (via your P.A.) because you were 'not there' at the time. But the impression will be that you are devoting yourself almost exclusively to the serious business of making money.

Routine administration takes up a great deal of time since it has to be done whether the business is making a lot of money or not. By relieving you of these tasks, the P.A. lets you get on with what you are supposed to be doing, even if this means that you end up helping the P.A. to do the work, rather than the other way round.

The Business Partner

Avoid having a business partner if you possibly can.

Indeed, given a choice between insolvency and a new partner, consider the former – it cuts out the middleman.

The Rest of the World

Everyone else falls into one of two categories:

1. **People who give you money** – customers and clients

2. **People you give money to** – suppliers, employees, advisers.

Both should be dealt with in exactly the same way. They must be approached with a display of self-confidence so absolute that they are forced to assume you must have something to be confident about.

If you can convince enough people, you may one day really have something to be confident about. On that day, when your small business is the big business it always pretended to be, you can admit how small you once were, and how you built your giant multi-national from a shed in your back garden.

Just make sure you don't tell anyone about the garden shed until it is safely buried in the concrete of your multi-storey head office.

GLOSSARY

If you ever want to be a big business, you have to talk like a big business from the start.

Major companies don't 'do' anything, they **'perform'** (as in "The company has performed well this year"). They don't 'have' anything, though they might **'enjoy'** something ("We* enjoyed a 50 per cent increase in sales"). They are not 'run', they **'operate'**. They are not 'helped by' anything, but they can **'benefit'** from something. They don't 'buy', but they do **'acquire'**. They don't 'make deals', they **'conduct transactions'**. Their figures 'say' nothing, but they may **'reflect'** something. Their problems and opportunities are not 'seen' but **'identified'**.

The following expressions might prove useful, if dropped in casual conversation.

unlimited opportunity for growth – the business is now at rock bottom.

room for improvement remains – it can't get any worse

disappointing results – total disaster

predict – hope for

expect – wish for

anticipate – pray for

imminent – you might just live to see it

put assets to work – sell off assets to cover losses

prioritise – cut

*Always use the Royal 'we', especially if there is only one of you.

57

selective purchasing – constant prioritising

prudent financial management – selective purchasing on a massive scale

rationalise – make excuses for

unique product – product no-one else is stupid enough to try to sell

temporary cash flow crisis – time to jump out of a top floor window

shortfall – long fall (usually by the Financial Director from a top floor window [see above])

market segmentation – the process of dividing humanity into the nice people who might buy one's product and the ungrateful scumbags who won't

cyclical market – why you are not to blame for the dramatic drop in sales

adverse market conditions – failed to sell anything

reactive marketing strategy – waiting to see what might turn up

opportunistic marketing strategy – hoping something will turn up

keeping all our options open – no strategy whatsoever

strategic – a useful prefix that can be placed in front of almost any business expression to make it sound more impressive without anyone being the wiser about what it actually means

improved performance – things didn't get noticeably worse

perceptible improvement – one you might just see if you look hard enough in the right place

notable improvement – one which you don't have to look too hard for

significant improvement – one so apparent that even an investor might notice it without your having to point it out more than six or seven times

healthy profits – any profits at all, unless they exceed all expectations [see below]

profits exceeded all our expectations – we accidentally made a profit when our accountant told us not to for tax reasons

interim dividend – a method of getting one's cash out of the business in a hurry

learning curve – why we have no idea what we are supposed to be doing

extended learning curve – why there is little prospect of us finding out what we are supposed to be doing in the near future

stable – stagnant

confident – truly desperate

exciting opportunity – long shot

considerable boost – lucky break

long-term prospects – the boss's favourite daydream

cautious but positive outlook – the directors are stiff with valium

redeployment – someone gets fired

restructuring – everyone gets fired

repositioning the business in the marketplace – looking for a completely different business to go into

diversifying – cutting one's losses in one's existing businesses

highly geared – heavily in debt

recapitalise for new development – get someone to extend our existing loans

expand overseas operations – seek some market, any market, that wants what we offer

increase overseas investments – leave the country (with the contents of all the company's bank accounts)

subject to macro-economic factors – totally out of control

slowdown in growth – dead stop and into reverse

economic downturn – business sinking fast

serious economic downturn – going under for the third time

severe economic downturn – glug, glug, glug

debtors – blood-sucking leeches who refuse to pay us

creditors – blood-sucking leeches who insist that we pay them

development plan – what we would do if only we had the money

increase in cash terms – decrease in real terms

rich in non-fiscal resources – no cash

increased asset value – we have a lot of unsold stock on our hands

tax purposes – ancient and mysterious incantation used by accountants when asked to justify their more illogical recommendations

Interest – money taken away from you when you don't have any

Income tax – money taken away from you when you eventually manage to make some at last

tax deductible – reason given for insisting that you keep anything that resembles a receipt, no matter how small the amount, whether you need to or not (even if you're not yet paying tax)

regrettable deviation from our usual high standard – we particularly regret that it was spotted

opportunity to liquidize previously committed assets – house repossessed

favourable long-term outlook – horrifying short-term outlook

the relevant statistic – the one that puts the business in the best light

the real issue – the one that enables you to quote the relevant statistic

broad-based approach – we haven't made up our minds yet

possible business contact – anyone you've ever heard of

good business contact – any possible business contact you've ever actually seen, heard, or spoken to, however briefly

networking – exploiting contacts ruthlessly

associate – good business contact who has been thoroughly networked

administration – paperwork

petty cash – contents of Boss's pocket

company reserves – contents of Boss's spouse's pocket

management accounts – back of the envelope in which one's bank statement came

management – the proper way of describing what any small business person actually does (as opposed to 'wheeling and dealing', the improper, albeit accurate, description)

Financial Director – book-keeper

Administrative Director – the Boss's P.A.

Marketing, Personnel, and R & D Director – the Boss's spouse (on the payroll for tax purposes)

customers – clients who insist on carrying something away in return for their money

clients – customers who are prepared to accept that you have given them something in return for their money without actually carrying it away

valued customer/client – one whose cheque didn't bounce

THE AUTHOR

John Winterson Richards has degrees in both law
(which he has ignored ever since) and business
administration (which taught him one valuable
lesson: the only people who make money through
MBAs are University Business Schools).

He is not, of course, a small businessman himself –
no definitely not – but an established and successful
leader of international commerce. If you have never
heard of him it is because, like all truly powerful
men, he likes to work behind the scenes.

His only connection with small business is through
Winterson Richards, the consultancy he founded to
help entrepreneurs less fortunate than himself. The
charitable nature of this operation explains the
ridiculously low fees it charges.

He is available for service as a Non-Executive
Director, at very reasonable rates, with a special
discount for companies operating in selected develop-
ing countries (such as Tahiti).

His ambition is to become one of the idle rich.
According to his friends, he is exactly half way there.

THE BLUFFER'S GUIDES®

Available at £1.99* and £2.99:

Accountancy
Astrology & Fortune Telling*
The Classics
Computers
Consultancy
Cricket
Doctoring
Economics
The European Union
The Flight Deck
Golf
The Internet
Journalism
Law
Management
Marketing
Men
Music
The Occult*
Opera

Personal Finance
Philosophy
Photography*
Public Relations
Public Speaking
The Quantum Universe
The Rock Business
Rugby
Science
Seduction
Sex
Skiing
Small Business
Stocks & Shares
Tax
Teaching
University
Whisky
Wine
Women